T0160904

Sanctuary

POEMS OF
LIFE AND LOVE

KATHRYN CAROLE ELLISON

Published by Lady Bug Books, an imprint of Brisance Books Group.
Lady Bug Press and the distinctive ladybug logo are registered trademarks of
Lady Bug Books, LLC.

Lady Bug Books
400 112th Avenue N.E.
Suite 230
Bellevue, WA 98004
www.ladybugbooks.net

For information about custom editions, special sales and permissions, please contact
Brisance Books Group at specialsales@brisancebooksgroup.com

Manufactured in the United States of America
ISBN: 978-1-944194-22-2

First Edition: June 2017

A NOTE FROM THE AUTHOR

The poems in this book were written over many, many years...
as gifts, of sorts, to my children. I began writing them in the
1970s, when my children were reaching the age of reason and
as I found myself in the position of becoming a single parent.
I needed something special to share with them—something that
would become a tradition, a ritual they could always count on...

And so the Advent Poems began—one day, decades ago—
with a poem 'gifted' to them each day during the December
holiday season every year. Forty years later... my children still
look forward to the poems that started a family tradition
that new generations have come to cherish.

It's my sincere hope that you will embrace and enjoy them
as we have and share them with those you love.

Children of the Light was among the first poems I wrote and
is included in each of the *Poems of Life and Love* books in
The Ellison Collection: *Heartstrings, Inspirations, Celebrations,
Sojourns, Awakenings,* and *Sanctuary.* After writing hundreds
of poems, it is still my favorite. The words came from my
heart and my soul and flowed so effortlessly that it was
written in a single sitting. All I needed to do was
capture the words on paper.

Light, to me, represented all that was good and pure and right
with the world, and I believed then—as I do today—that those
elements live in my children... and perhaps in all of us.
We need only to dare...

– KCE

DEDICATION

To my parents: Herb and Bernice Haas

Mom, you were the poet who went before me...
unpublished, but appreciated nonetheless.

And Dad, you always believed in me,
no matter what direction my life took.
Thank you for your faith in me,
and for your unconditional love.

TABLE OF CONTENTS

LIFE'S JOYS

LIFE'S LESSONS

LIFE'S GIFTS

LIFE'S JOYS

PEACE

Peace is the state to which people aspire.
The path is thought to be lonely and long,
But the surprising fact is that one can achieve it
Only through people! Forging alone is wrong.

It's true! All alone, peace is not guaranteed.
It's dependent entirely on ˈthe dance,ˈ
With skills such as tact and patience thrown in,
And open-mindedness to see every stance.

It's putting the power of goodwill to work.
It's using sanity, maturity, and common sense.
It is vision, it's taking a long, careful look
Before jumping to one side or the other of a fence.

Peace is straight thinking. Avoid negative thoughts.
They are mental webs of prejudice and fear.
Cut through those webs in your interactions.
That's the goal that peace lovers hold dear.

Peace is a quality of the heart and the head.
It needs both together, working hand and glove.
It's a warmth, a joy of living that reaches out
And draws people together with love.

KNOW YOURSELF

When you are in touch with who you are
And what you represent and believe,
Any need to search for something else
To define you will up and leave!

Like feelings of happiness or sadness,
Self-knowledge is an 'inside job.'
Nobody else can define who you are.
If you let them, they'll only rob
You of your potential to grow beyond
The limiting definition they attach.
Don't be dragged away from who you are.
Those naysayers you must simply dispatch.

For you are a work that deserves the best –
The time, attention, and a willing attitude
To grow and blossom, to your life's potential.
Know yourself to the fullest magnitude.

NATURE

Nature is not only an environment I live in,
But an aspect of myself expressed throughout.
It's the teacher that constantly awakens me
To beauty, harmony and transformation all about.

It reminds me of our total interconnectedness
To all which inhabits this planet of ours.
It allows me the chance to care for all that lives
As if it were myself. I have those powers.

After looking for differences I finally saw 'same.'
Nature patiently taught me; I was able to see.
To paraphrase Pogo from funny-paper fame,
'I went out to find (nature) and discovered it was me.'

LOVE

Love turns on the sun every morning of our lives.
It lets us know all is well with the world.
All of our cares of days gone by
Disappear as away they are hurled.

Only love can bring out man's full potential.
(Women are included in this generality.)
It discovers within our ambitions and goodness
And makes them a living reality.

Love multiplies an energy beyond imagination.
It keeps us going after others drop.
Love excites courage to match any warrior's.
It takes us to a mountaintop.

Love allows us to face anything life has to offer,
No matter the severity of the claim.
It protects us from things unknown to us now.
It affords endurance of scandal and shame.

Love gives us solace when we are in need.
It refreshes like gentle rain on our brow.
It takes away the fears of the past or the future,
And lets us live in the now.

Love's fires glow the brightest, its arrows are sharp.
It speaks a language known to lovers alone.
Love is the answer no matter the question.
Our remarkable loving power we must own.

BE HERE NOW

"Be Here Now," the Man said; He knew the secret
Of how best to live one's life;
Of how to move from day to day
Without any trouble and strife.
Yet He gave us all minds with which to think,
And those minds can lead us in any direction.
The secret of using our minds, my loves,
Is with temperance, and in connection
With our hearts and our bodies and with our souls,
Maintaining balance as we go along the way.
When we do, we're happy, and things go well.
When we don't, we're off center, and we pay.

We pay in ways we can't even describe
To ourselves and to others around us.
We just know something's amiss, it doesn't feel good,
And we cry and complain and cuss.

When that happens, and it does, to the best now and then
There's only one thing we can do:
Take time out, take a break, and think of the whole...
And to ourselves be true...
Not to the ego self, oh no, my word,
That's the thing that brought on the trouble;
But the Whole Self that speaks with an inner voice,
And you'll come back on the double
To an inner peace, a feeling of love,
A centering that is in the present.
And then you'll know the meaning of the words,
"Be Here Now." It's very pleasant.

CONSTANCY

If it is success you are seeking, then listen to these words:
(They will help to form your thinking. They will give you a clue.)
In order to succeed at whatever you are attempting,
Constancy to purpose wins. The onus is on you.

Intellect and cleverness are not to be dismissed
As factors which contribute to the reaching of your goal.
But without the direction and constancy of your will
All the ideas in the world are not diamonds; they are coal!

Discipline provides the constancy to stay focused
On any goal you choose to pursue to its end.
By staying on firm ground you can deal with any stresses
That come your way. Your doubts you can transcend.

COURTING ADMIRATION

What is the point of courting admiration?
It's not a good reason to perform.
What others praise today, they may condemn tomorrow;
To their "rules" you need not conform.

Yes, kudos are nice; applause is great.
There's no one who would disagree.
But framing your behavior for approval alone
Puts your soul in jeopardy.

Seek, rather, to shine before your own conscience.
Be a star where it really counts.
Do what's right – but right, for you alone,
Take authenticity into account!

BEING HUMAN

There's a lot more to being human
Than bumping along a road.
It requires attention to detail
As you travel with your load.

You need to affirm that you are proud
To be part of the human race,
And proud that you live together with
All species, and colors of face.

The goodness of God can be known only
Through sharing with others on earth.
It takes courage and kindness... humility, too –
Virtues you've practiced since birth.

To absorb life as it comes to you,
Changing whatever you cannot abide;
Adapting yourself to what is unyielding
And learning to live alongside.

To admit it is possible you've made a mistake,
Then learning instead of repeating;
Being patient with others when they are in error,
Then forgiving, with no tempers heating.

To share courage and hope with all you meet;
To share laughter and the accompanying wit;
To live in the present – let the future unfold
Exactly as Nature intends it.

To be grateful for the precious gift of life
With its limitless opportunities for all;
And to glory in the power of humans to rise
To great heights upon receipt of the call.

THE PARADOX OF LETTING GO

"When I let go of what I am
I become what I might be.
When I let go of what I have,
I receive what I need."

Struggling for work or love, it seems,
Often pushes your reality elsewhere.
But when you give up the struggle and relax,
You find what you want suddenly there.

"When I give of myself
I become more.
When I feel most destroyed
I am about to grow.
When I desire nothing
A great deal comes to me."

Wanting freedom and independence
There is no need to claw...
The very best way to achieve your goal
Is to conform to the Natural Law.

"My best work is done when I
Forget my own point of view
The less I make of myself,
The more I am."

When you try to make yourself look good
The act is too aggressive.
Give up trying to impress anyone else,
And you become VERY impressive.

CHILDREN OF THE LIGHT

There are those souls who bring the light,
Who spill it out for all to share.
And with a joy that does excite,
They show the world that they do care.
It is so very bright.

In this sharing, love does pervade
Into their lives and cycles round;
And as this light is outward played
The love is also inward bound.
It is an awesome trade.

You are a soul whose light is shared.
It comes from deep within your heart.
It's best because it is not spared,
Because it's total, not just part.
And I am glad you've dared.

Optimism

Optimism is the faith that leads to achievement.
Nothing can be done without confidence and hope.
Faith is a passionate intuition you possess;
Against all odds and setbacks you will cope.
Faith will give you an inner strength, a confidence...
A sense of balance and ability to keep things in scope.

Faith is a knowledge within your heart
That reaches beyond any limits of evidence.
It is reason grown courageous; a state of openness and trust,
And the principal part of faith is patience.
With faith you can trust without reservation.
Believe in yourself; you'll move forward with confidence.

MAKING YOUR OWN DECISIONS

The craving for self-esteem can be addictive
If measured by external standards.
It's elusive, fickle, and like any drug
Can lead you to want more... awards?

True self-esteem comes from setting your own sails,
And from making your own decisions;
Then acting on the choices you make,
Leaving room for your own revisions.

Fear of making the wrong choice can be great,
And for some, too tough to consider.
So they yield to others their power to choose
And live their life as an outsider.

Letting others make our choices for us
Is a whole growth industry today.
Psychic hotlines and spirit mediums
Guide our choices, and it's we who pay.

Don't ask others to tell you what to do.
Take ownership of your decision-making.
It's a beautiful world when you're open to choose;
And it's there, my dears, for the taking.

PANTHEISM

Realizing...
Realizing that I am...
I am a part of everything...
Everything that is sustained by the power of creation...
The power that brought the very universe into existence!
I must open my heart to life!
I am not a lonely planet!
I am not alone... I am
Part of it all...
Is it?
It is.
True.

LIFE'S LESSONS

DETERMINATION

A dream doesn't become a reality through magic.
It takes sweat, determination and hard work.
The determination to win is the better part of winning...
Each step is important, so do not shirk.

Get up every morning with the determination to succeed
In order to go to bed each night with satisfaction.
An invincible determination can accomplish about anything.
Positive energy toward your work is an attraction.

You can have all the talent in the world, you know;
Without determination to succeed, it is wasted.
And nobody else can give you determination, oh no!
It must come from within; then success will be tasted.

Desire is the key to motivation, my friends,
But determination and commitment to your goal
Will enable you to attain the success you seek.
And success breeds success, as a whole.

The truest wisdom is a resolute determination
To stay focused in spite of interference.
It's not having mighty strength that gets the job done...
Great works are performed by perseverance.

TRUST YOUR INNER VOICE

It's said that the way we talk to our children
Becomes the voice they hear inside.

The most influential voice you ever will hear
Is that one that resides inside your heart.
It can work in your favor, or it can bring downfall,
Depending on the message it does impart.

Choose to listen to your own inner voice,
Not the jumbled opinions of those around you.
Do what you know in your heart is right.
Your inner voice will guide you through.

Always do your best to be yourself!
Learn to listen to your inner voice.
It's your true authenticity – who you really are...
Strive to reach your destiny, and rejoice.

It's said there are four things to value in your life:
Your Family is the first; you are born with the choice.
Your Self-Respect, and your Dignity follow;
And the last is to value your Inner Voice.

All the wonders you seek are within yourself.
You contain within you the Holy Grail.
It's your obligation to find your own treasure.
Look inside, heed your voice, and you will not fail.

YOU ARE YOUR ENVIRONMENT

The first step you make toward getting somewhere
Is to be dissatisfied staying where you are.
You alone make the world you live in,
And you bring your environment up to par.

Avoid people who'd belittle your ambition.
(Small people are famous for this.)
Successful people will make you feel
That you, too, can thrive... that you just can't miss!

Your environment is your natural feeding ground
From which your desire to succeed does come.
Choose your environment and make it positive.
It lifts you up and empowers wisdom.

THE REAL YOU

If you don't know yourself and your charms,
Or faults (that's 'eccentricities,' of course),
You cannot present your authentic self.
You must access your nature, and its source.

If you allow others to define you,
As some are determined to do,
It can leave you empty and dejected.
You must stop them before they are through.

If you know yourself to be strong and durable,
You'll face whatever your life brings.
You need not fear the challenges you'll face;
You'll have many more happy endings.

DUST OFF YOUR DREAMS

As each year rolls around to your birthday,
It's a good time to take an inventory
So you can begin, renewed and free,
From repeating the same old story.

Looking to the past gives a guide to our future.
It's a good time to sort out the negative.
Seek out perfection, toss those old resentments and fears,
And give yourself a new directive.

A time to examine the things left undone
And to do something about them – now...
To make that visit or finish that task...
To examine your life and reavow.

Renewal allows you to dust off your dreams:
To polish your ideals once again.
To see were you are and where you want to go,
And to go forward with a grin.

A time to reread those precious old books
And letters that have brought so much pleasure...
A time to give thanks for all that you are
And all that you have to treasure.

It's a time to resolve to add life to your years,
A time of rededication
To things that endure: The great use of life
Is spent on constant self-creation.

BACKWARDS THROUGH THE MIRROR

It's not that others' qualities be real
Or that they live up to some high ideal.
What others do is not my main concern.
I needn't label shortcomings with zeal
Or, Goodness knows, belabor with a spiel.
It's from their acts that I am made to learn.

And in these acts I see what I admire –
It is to these good virtues I aspire.
There is so much to do right here inside.
The qualities that I wish to acquire
Need constant testing in the hottest fire.
The work is hard, there is no place to hide.

So, what the other fellow does is fine
And my job is to keenly toe my line.
I do not judge the other person's goal.
My time is spent on bringing out the shine,
And burnishing those traits that I call mine.
It's comforting to comprehend my role.

DO WE NEED PROOF?

Do we need proof that we are essential;
That we alone appease some needs;
And so exist to be a functionary –
The doer of our share of good deeds?

In all the world, no one can take our place.
Nobody else can ever be like us.
We're special because we embrace this life
And emanate our love. It is quite glorious.

Our feelings, in their swinging back and forth,
Can be seen as a cause to celebrate.
Feelings are the sign we use to measure worth:
Just being alive is our proof ultimate.

FORGIVING IS NOT FORGETTING

How can the human mind hang on to all it does
Without a breaking down along the way?
Things happen – the mind records all that occurs
And then it's time for you to have a say.

If what has happened causes pain or grief to you,
Then that's the time when you can make a choice.
You either just accept what 'fate' has dealt to you
Or you speak out for you in your strong voice.

What follows then to ease the mind is to forgive,
Though things may not return to status quo.
Forgiving does not mean forgetting all that's done –
It is remembering, and then letting go.

WORDS

Your words should be music to another's ears.
Be sure to weigh them as though they were gold.
Have love in your heart for yourself and others
When in conversation your opinions unfold.

You are what you say, because you are
What you are thinking all the day long.
Keep positive thoughts, discard the rest
And in your heart always sing a song.

Your life and your words, your words and your life;
They will go hand in hand... forever.
You cannot be careless with one, and then
Try to be overly careful with the other.

A word rightly spoken can renew someone,
But careless words may often bring pain.
Words that come off the top of your head
Have probably not even passed through your brain.

Remember to make your words light enough
To float another's spirit, and change his role;
And also to make them weighty enough
To sink to the very bottom of his soul.

DUTY CALLS

Authentic freedom places demands on us,
Though some often think it means doing as they like.
But those who put their feelings before basic reason
Are actually slaves to their desires and dislikes.

Look at it this way: we're not isolated,
But an irreplaceable piece of the cosmos.
Our job is to find out where we fit in,
Then live in relation to others, to the utmost.

Our duties emerge rather naturally
Based on our place with family and friends,
And with our workplace, our state, and our nation.
Consider your roles. They're not hard to comprehend.

Once you know who you are and to whom
You are linked, you will know what to do.
Keep to your higher purpose, seek balance with nature.
This is the road to harmony that is true.

Other people cannot hurt you, unless you allow it,
Even though it seems to be their main goal.
Do not feel victimized by their words or deeds.
It is a choice over which you have control.

STRESS TEST
OR STRESS-LESS *OR* STRESS LESS

Massages, walks on the beach, or ferry rides...
Funny movies, hot baths, or the park and slides...
These things and more can reduce our stress.
Why don't we think of them when we're under duress?

Cups of hot cocoa to drink when it's cold...
A pause from our labors without being told...
These things and more can reduce our stress.
Why don't we think of them when we're under duress?

Planning ahead for free time in our day...
Being sure we take it and let nothing block the way...
These things and more can reduce our stress.
Why don't we think of them when we're under duress?

LIFE'S GIFTS

GOD'S GIFT

YOU ARE...
Capable of being your own best friend,
And when you forget it you suffer.
But when you remember to love you first,
A wonderful person you encounter.

GOD'S...
Instructions to you are to live each day
Using what abilities you have for His tasks...
And when you think highly of what you can do
There is no longer the need for masks.

GIFT...
Is defined as that which is given...
It's described as power or talent.
The power is there to be tapped at will;
All it takes is self-acknowledgement.

TO YOU...
The gifts of God's love are abundant,
They're at hand; they're there for the taking.
When you no longer block your own path through life
You'll find joy in the progress you're making.

TRUE TO YOURSELF

The most common regret of people approaching death
Is lamenting the lack of courage
To have lived a life of being true to themselves.
Those who do have a distinct advantage.

Living a life that others choreograph,
If not true to your own dreams and wishes,
Is no life at all – no matter how ˙posh.˙
Your life is your own to establish.

The choices you make will guide your life.
By honoring your dreams you stay true
To yourself and to others who are in your life.
Being true to yourself is a virtue!

MEDITATION MINDSET

The mind gets so busy! My thoughts are jumbled!
I can't decide which way to turn first.
Does this happen to you? Is it driving you mad?
The times when this happens are the worst!

It just means you've strayed from your Spiritual Self;
You've let yourself and others block the path back.
Twenty minutes a day in quiet meditation
Can be helpful to getting back on track.

You'll feel healthier and less stressed
Than you have felt before!
You'll be inspired with the results,
And keep going back for more.

HONOR

There's only one person in your life whose respect
You must seek to gain, at all hazards and harm.
'Cause when it is present you are second to none;
Your feelings will become comfortable and warm.

You room with the person and walk with the person;
You work, eat and sleep with the person, too.
If you haven't already figured it out,
The person in question can be only you!

Nothing in life will bring satisfaction
Unless you have honor and self-respect.
Honor will bring more joy than wealth or fame
And on other's lives you'll have a positive effect.

Honesty lends honor, of that there's no doubt.
Integrity comes from being honest inside.
To gain honor from others for anything
You cannot from the truth ever hide.

It will seek you out from any hiding place
That you might ever try to find;
And expose any lack of honesty, then
Show you the way – because love is kind.

GRACE

Grace is not a part of consciousness.
It is neither knowledge nor reason.
It is the amount of light present in your soul
That you carry with you every season.

It has been defined as the outward expression
Of the inward harmony of the soul.
There's an air of mystery about what grace is.
It is something you do not control.

Like many things in life, the attainment of grace
Does not come with an owner's manual.
It is not achieved by following step-by-step lessons.
And it can disappear without any signal.

Grace is achieved when you are your own true self;
When your inner- and your outer-selves are one...
When you live your life being true to your nature;
When your deeds match your thoughts... well done!

Always have humility when you create,
And grace when you succeed.
It's not about you... you are the terminal
For a higher power in the lead.

FRIENDS

Friends are people you make part of your life
Just because it feels good;
Not because you happen to be related,
Or live close, or think you should.

You say you like someone because
Your passions are the same.
You both read the same kind of books,
Or play a certain board game.

It's comfortable when your friends do share
What tickles your particular fancy;
But as a requirement to be your friend
It carries little relevancy.

The job you do, the way you vote –
Matters not at all to a friend.
On what you've accomplished or where you've failed,
Your friendship doesn't depend.

The usual distinctions of older–younger
Or richer–poorer, and like that,
Are gone as you meet with a fresh clean slate
On equal terms to chat.

Basically, your friends are not your friends
For any particular reason.
They're just your friends; and friends they stay,
No matter what the season.

SUCCESS

Measuring success in terms of praise
Or lack thereof throughout your days

Will cause anxiety beyond belief,
And pain for which there's no relief.

If you're applauded for what you do
And you feel good, as you're likely to,

Just know the next time they're likely not
To match the volume that first you got.

And worse to think they might next criticize
And question your actions with lots of 'whys.'

What then will you do... feel hurt? You might
If you are dependent on others casting light.

PICTURE YOUR OWN EVOLUTION

How you see yourself is in your own mind,
Not to be reflected from another's view.
In a positive or a negative vision of self –
The choice is simply up to you.

Your freedom comes not from someone else.
It comes from your own resolve
To stand up for what you believe in your heart.
It's the best way for you to evolve.

KEEP YOUR WISHES REAL

In order to be truly free
We must take stock of two or three
Of the natural laws in the universe:
Immutable, unchangeable, somewhat terse.

For good or ill, life and nature
Are governed by immutable laws.
Accepting this truth will ease your mind
When you're bothered and don't know the cause.

It's impossible for any of us to live forever:
The law of immortality is out of our hands.
And wishing others to be without fault
Is like building a structure on shifting sands.

It's within our control to shape our desires,
Based on facts rather than on an emotional wave.
For freedom, wish for nothing that depends on others,
If you do, you will be a helpless slave.

Freedom's not the right to do whatever you please.
It's from understanding limits, both your own and those divine;
And accepting those limits and working with them.
Keep these simple steps in mind and you'll be fine.

DARING TO LOVE

An often-missed challenge when you love –
That is, when you love another wholly –
Is the art of being a ˚coequal˚ partner,
Not giving – or exacting – your love solely.

The challenge is to give up your old ideas
Of behaving a certain way as your love grows;
Deciding to be neither master nor servant
As you face all of your tomorrows.

You are partners as you dance along life's trail.
You are equal in every want and need.
One cannot ask for more than his or her due,
Nor give up self – the love won't succeed.

The line is fine, as dancers know well;
To the music they apply motion.
The moves each make affect the other's step
And each responds to changes in emotion.

And so this love entails the greatest risk,
That of baring one's self, heart and soul;
To be completely open and sincere,
When caution says we must use self-control.

TAKING TIME TO LIVE

To get the most out of life, you need balance between
Taking time to live and making a living.
When your life is all work, with no time to reflect
There's not much to draw from for giving.

Time for good books and good music to wash
Away from the soul all the dust...
Time for friendships and talks and walks;
Time for children from whom you learn trust...

Time for laughter and letting go
Of all the cares you carry around...
Time for travel and seeing new things,
Whether by air or water or ground.

Nature beckons when you take time to live,
With her splendorous works of art.
To frolic among the beauty on earth
Is good for the soul and the heart.

Take time to love and be loved in return,
For love is the greatest gift you know.
Take time, as well, for exchanging ideas;
That's the best way to learn and grow.

Take time to give of yourselves, your talents,
That you contribute to the march of man,
And raise the level of understanding and truth
To the highest you possibly can.

CLEAR YOUR CALENDAR

It's easy to fill your calendar with events
Which require your attendance and dollars.
But be careful to keep ample time for yourself...
The obligations can feel like tight collars.

It's when you are quiet, and sometimes alone
Or with loved ones close to your heart
That real communion takes place and the spirit is felt;
That the glow of inspiration can create art.

If you're over-scheduled and constantly running
Here and there, there and here, and back.
You'll miss the life-altering gifts which abound;
They'll come to you when you relax.

Make space in your life for no action at all!
Make leisure time part of your daily routine.
Let the Spirit in and listen to the message,
And enjoy those times serene.

A CLOSING THOUGHT

POETRY

It's the revelation
Of a sensation
That the poet
(Wouldn't you know it)
Believes to be
Felt only interiorly
And personal to
The writer who
... writes it.

It's the interpretation
Of a sensation
That was fueled by
A poet's sigh
And believed to be
Shared mutually
And personal to
The lucky one who
... reads it.

About the Author

Kathryn Carole Ellison is a former newspaper columnist
and journalist and, of course, a poet.

She lives near her children and stepchildren and their families in the
Pacific Northwest, and spends winters in the sunshine of Arizona.

You might find her on the golf course with friends, river rafting,
writing poems... or at the opera.

Late Bloomer

Our culture honors youth with all
It's unbridled effervescence.
We older ones sit back and nod
As if in acquiescence.

And when our confidence really gels
In early convalescence...
'We can't be getting old!' we cry,
'We're still struggling with adolescence!'

Acknowledgments

I have many people to thank...

First of all, my children Jon and Nicole LaFollette, for inspiring the writing of these poems in the first place. And for encouraging me to continue my writing, even though their wisdom and compassion surpass mine.

My wonderful stepchildren, Debbie and John Bacon, Jeff and Sandy Ellison, and Tom and Sue Ellison, who, with their children and grandchildren, continue to be a major part of my life and are loved deeply by me. These poems are for you, too.

Eva LaFollette, the dearest daughter-in-law one could ever wish for... and one of my dearest friends. Your encouragement and interest are so appreciated.

My good friends who have received a poem or two of mine in their Christmas cards these many years, for complimenting me on the messages in my poems. Your encouragement kept me writing.

To Kim Kiyosaki who introduced me to the right person to get the publishing process underway... that person being Mona Gambetta with Brisance Books Group who has the experience and know-how to make these books happen.

And finally, to John Laughlin, a fellow traveler in life, who encourages me every day in the writing and publishing process. John, I love having you in my cheering section!

Other books

by Kathryn Carole Ellison

Awakenings

Sojourns

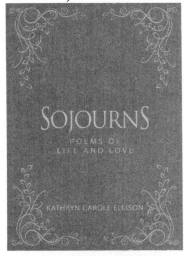

Heartstrings

Inspirations

Celebrations